APOLOGY TO HUGH & ROBERT, KINGS OF FRANCE

St. Abbo of Fleury

Translated by: D.P. Curtin

APOLOGY TO HUGH & ROBERT, KINGS OF FRANCE

Copyright @ 2006 Dalcassian Publishing Company

All rights reserved. No part of this publication may be reproduced, distributed, or transmitted in any form or by any means, including photocopying, recording, or other electronic or mechanical methods, without the prior written permission of the publisher, except in the case of brief quotations embodied in critical reviews and certain other non-commercial uses permitted by copyright law. For permission request, write to Dalcassian Publishing Company at dalcassianpublishing at gmail.com

ISBN: 979-8-8692-1003-6 (Paperback)

Library of Congress Control Number:
Author: Curtin, D.P. (1985-)

Printed by Ingram Content Group, 1 Ingram Blvd, La Vergne, Tennessee

First printing edition 2006.

APOLOGY TO HUGH & ROBERT, KINGS OF FRANCE

APOLOGY TO HUGH & ROBERT, KINGS OF FRANCE

Apology to Hugh & Robert, Kings of France

It often happens that, while the mind is exhausted by the horror of the calamities of the insurgents, the troubled mind does not by the horror itself prepare what it ought to have said, but, carried away by the phantasm of thoughts elsewhere, says what ought to be kept silent, and, as a consequence, keeps silent about what needs to be said. For he always loves the rest of the utmost tranquility, who has managed to arrange the secret of truth by reasoning: therefore from the very rudiments of discipline, as a deer longs for springs of water (Ps. 41:1), so my soul longed for the laborious leisure of spiritual philosophy that I might turn into an honest business for the benefit of many ; but, having been hindered by my sins, and having left him, I have in a way been reduced to the anxiety of the world, who, under the care of the pastoral government, daily sustains me with the water of distress and the bread of tribulation (3 Kings 22, 27): the supplanting cunning of my rivals gnaws at me with the canine tooth of my rivals, the frequent bitterness of my adversaries barks around me, and they murmured nothing against me, except that I wished the senate of monks to be safe, I sought the increase of our republic, and I contradicted the scorn of those who were lying in wait by the authority with which I prevailed, and I did not at all conceal mercy and truth from the council. For such evils as these they lie in wait for my blood, they pursue me with hatred, so much so that even the royal majesty does not deter them from slaughtering me with a club, if the place or the time laughs at them. Wherefore in my prayers I beseech God diligently to judge and discern my cause as usual, and to deliver me from the wicked and deceitful man (Ps. 42:1); and if I take the place of defending myself before my lord bishops, whom I learned to be orthodox in the Catholic faith, I believe that I will be harmless from the crime if they examine the origin of the quarrels without accepting persons. For who, with his own prejudice, would come to this, that any of the possessions of the monastery should be alienated? What twister of facts and twister of laws presumes to confuse the cords of ecclesiastical inheritance by mixing them, when it is written: Do not transgress the boundaries which your fathers have set? (Prov. 22, 22.) Behold, according to the rules of the holy Fathers, subject to the judgment of the bishops, I do not flee the audience, I will give an account of my stewardship, so much so that I accept it in faith so as not to be intercepted by those who lie in wait and suffer anything; who am ready to die, if at any time I commit myself to a worthy death. And first of all I wish to discuss my faith, without which I cannot be saved, so that by my examination others may succeed, or by my remonstrance they may know that they have fallen into heresy, from which they shall try as much as possible to be freed: lest, by remaining in it until death, they become the devil's stalk; for whoever believes otherwise about God, about religion, about the common state of the holy Church than what Christ taught, or what the Catholic Church held under the holy apostles and handed down to his successors, is not a Catholic or a believer, but is clearly a heretic. For all heretics were so persecuted by our fathers, that at the beginning, when the faith was exposed, they examined in their councils lest any should feel anything contrary to the apostles themselves, who, being discovered, without any delay, was either brought back to the body of the whole Church, or, even to the renunciation of error, shocked by anathema, deprived of Catholicism it is communion, and the orthodox no more avoided touching a serpent than clinging to a contaminated leprosy of this kind. Hence we are forbidden in the canons, if we know ourselves to be Catholics, not to at least pray with them. The pious prince, out of the abundance of his possessions, provided abundantly for the expense of driving away from him all the heretics, that is, those who in word or deed felt differently from the holy apostles. When this was done, the purity of the pious faith pleased the prince to such an extent that he himself and his wife, under this signature, publicly profess it before that great council, whose pious religion you should imitate, our lords, Hugh and Robert, most illustrious kings, if you wish to be heirs to Christ in the land of the living. and unite yourselves, and drive out of your kingdom all heretical perversion, that God may keep you in eternal peace. Indeed, it must be known that the priest intercedes every day between the solemnities of the masses, not for heretics or schismatics, but only for the orthodox and worshipers of the Catholic and Apostolic faith, supplicating to God, from which supplication there is of course a stranger who divides himself in word or deed by being proud of their unanimity; but he who humbly confesses that he is burdened with sins, or doubts his faith, is to be borne and corrected, not as a stranger, but as a brother, because not even while he took his part with the hypocrites, especially when Peter, the leader of the Church, denied God, and Thomas doubted his faith; indeed, we know that there are three orders, as if three degrees, of both sexes of the faithful in the holy and universal Church; of whom, although none is without sin, yet the first is good, the second better, the third the best. And indeed it is the first order in both sexes of the married; the second of the continent, or widows; a third of virgins or saints. There are likewise three degrees or orders of men, the first of which is that of the laity, the second of the clergy, and the third of the monks. But since I have set forth the differences of these degrees, and have led the way to say that one is better or more holy than another, how each one in his purpose expects the reward of eternal retribution, or how they can be promoted from one degree to another by the authority of the holy Fathers, I thought it expedient briefly.

And in the matter of marriage only indulgence is permitted, lest by the frailty of the flesh it should be dragged down into a worse age. For no one is forbidden to marry, except he who, for the sake of earning the joys of the heavenly country, has voluntarily chosen a yoke of self-control, which, even if he has exhibited less, must be destroyed by a more secret devotion, a more secret deed, by penitence; but if the priests of the Old Testament wished to defend this to themselves, falling to their own level, they shed their guilt with tears. Here is the reason: if it is among those to whom it is lawful, no penalty is imposed, but it is also considered worthy of a reward, because in obedience, it is content with the chastity which the Apostle taught; and for this reason it is added if it is among those to whom it is lawful, because there are in both sexes who bind themselves by a vow that, if they are virgins, they may continue in virginity; and, if they are not virgins, they live in celibacy perpetually in contempt of the union of the flesh; it is also kinship or kinship of a kind, from the carnal commingling of which all who are under the Catholic faith are prohibited. Moreover, among those who bind themselves by a vow, or among those who have not passed the seventh line of descent, an abominable marriage must be dissolved immediately under the remedy of penance, just as that which does not require penance, because it is permitted by authority, must never be dissolved, unless either by the death of the other spouse, or both celibates by profession.

From here we pass to the more excellent order of widows or widows, in which, according to the Apostle, if they remain, they will deserve a crown of eternal reward so much as they endure a heavier punishment for the pleasure of the flesh. He also indulged them in a second marriage out of discretion, saying that it was better to marry than to burn (1 Cor. 7:9). As for third or fourth marriages, or even several marriages, I do not remember having read whether they should be celebrated by Catholics; but this occurs without any scruple: for if this deed is serious in women, it is much more serious if it happens to men.

No one is ignorant of the great glory of virgins. Who knows that man desires this from the prerogative grace which an angel has by nature? which virtue of virginity, when it is consolidated in humility, will be given as a reward of singular merit, because God promises virgins that they will follow the Lamb wherever he goes (Rev. 14:4); The venerable college is decorated with this virtue of the saints, and many rejoice that they have earned it in all the manly ranks in the bosom of their mother Church.

But to these postulates, first of the order of men, that is, of the laity, it must be said that some are farmers, others laborers; but the agonists, contented with military campaigns, do not collide in their mother's womb, but attack with all sagacity the adversaries of the holy Church of God.

The order of clerics follows, which is especially distinguished in three degrees, that is, deacons, priests, and bishops: for all those who are of a lower degree are called clerics by abuse, while they, like the laity, are permitted by indulgence to associate with spouses. It is clear that the apostles and their successors prohibited clerics, that is, deacons, priests, and bishops, from marrying. 'Κλῆρος', indeed, in Greek, is called 'lot' in Latin, whence clerics who are drawn into the lot of God to sacrifice or minister should strive to beget children not carnally but spiritually, so that they may always be mindful of the lot of the saints in the light. For they themselves, taken up by the daily concern of all the Churches (2 Cor. 2, 28), labor in an active life with Martha, who is troubled towards many (Luke 10, 41). Moreover, that one thing which is necessary in the contemplative life of monks who have attained, with Mary, they delight so much more to water the feet of Jesus with tears and to wipe their hair (Luke 7:38), the more they are removed from the restlessness of all the affairs of the world. As much as the superior is inferior, so much is inferior to the superior, since it is joined to the other by what differs from each order. For they are united to their spouses, devoted to the care of their family affairs, occupied with the deeds of the world: these are alienated from the deeds of the world, renouncing their own will, obeying the commands of the spiritual Father, who live by the alms of good men and by the labor of their hands, and can say with Peter: Behold, we have left us everything, and we have followed you (Matt. 19:27). Finally, the life of the clerics is an irreproachable mirror of the whole Church, just as the habits and firm profession of the monks are an example of the highest penitence of all; and although clerics worthy of censure, lest they treat holy things profanely, are degraded for certain reasons, yet monks, except for pride, are never deprived of the whole communion of their brethren, when they also take in criminals, laymen or clerics, and when they are caught in crime they rebuke them with regular discipline. Finally, a priest ordained from among monks, or a monk made from a cleric, should know that he does not serve ecclesiastical offices in the manner of clerics, but celebrates masses in the congregation by the institution of the Gregorian privilege. It is true that since what seemed to have been said about each order, it is not necessary to remain silent as to how one is promoted to another. For they are promoted from the laity or clerics to the monasticate, they are promoted from the laity or monks to the clergy, which the authority of the holy Fathers makes clear when or how it should be done, that those who did not follow outside the Catholic Church strayed from the faith. Wherefore in the canon, while they pray for the orthodox and the worshipers of the Catholic and Apostolic faith, they must be warned above all that Pope Gregory reports in his synod: There is one faith, he says, one baptism, one Catholic Church, in which alone sins can be expunged. For if there is no remission of sins outside of it, why should a heretic or schismatic fast? So what does he give tithes? So what God does the suppliant worship? For just as the multitude of believers had one heart and one soul (Acts 4:32), so, throughout the whole world, of all those who, according to the teaching of the apostles, have one wisdom in God, there is one Church, which is translated from the Greek into the Latin convocation, because we are all called to one faith and one baptism. For this reason, every house where the people gather to supplicate God at an erected altar, as long as it has the name of the church, is worthy of veneration and the highest honor in every nation, because in it we are reborn from water and the Holy Spirit (John 3:5), in it the divine mysteries are celebrated. in it the confession and remission of sins is made. Whoever, therefore, wishes to be saved, should be careful not to believe that it belongs to anyone but God alone; whence it is said to Peter, the chief of the apostles: You are Peter, and upon this rock I will build my Church (Matt. 16:18). He says mine, not yours; and Christ elsewhere: My house shall be called the house of prayer (Matt. 21:13). The psalmist also: Holiness befits your house, O Lord (Ps. 92:5). If then the Church is not Peter's, whose will it be? or will the successors of Peter dare to claim for themselves a power which Peter, the leader of the Church, did not have? Certainly, dear princes, we neither live Catholic nor speak Catholic, when I say that church is mine, he says the other is his, and like some cattle compared to foolish cattle, we sometimes offer both for sale, and we are not afraid to buy those proposed by others.

There is also another most serious error, in which it is said that the altar is the bishop's, and the church belongs to any other lord, when from the consecrated house and the altar one thing is made which is called the church, just as one man consists of body and soul. See, most righteous princes, whither greed leads us, while charity cools us (Matt. 24:12); from the gifts of Almighty God, which are freely received, we become merchants, and we try to sell what we certainly do not possess. For it seems that almost nothing pertains to the Church, which is of God alone, that is not given at a price, namely, the episcopate, the presbyterate, the diaconate, and the other lesser degrees, the archdeaconry also, the deanery, the presbytery, the custody of the treasury, the baptistery, the burial, and if there are any of the like . And businessmen of this kind, with a subtle answer, usually pretend that they are not buying the blessing by which the grace of the Holy Spirit is perceived, but the things of the Churches, or the possessions of the bishop, since it is certain that in the Catholic Church one cannot do without the other. Has anyone used fire without the material by which it is fueled? or did he sometimes hold the fire, and lacked the heat? Who is honey without sweetness? Who has discovered absinthe without bitterness? However, it is possible to find the same water sweet and bitter in different contents; which, because it comes from the contingent, sometimes misleads our opinion, so that what is believed to be sweet, exists bitter. In this way, too, such a business is considered good, when it is certainly bad, because it involves the grace of filthy lucre: in which matter the custom has become so ingrained, that it is now believed that this can be done without sin. True, the Holy Spirit says through the mouth of the blessed Pope Gregory: Because a blessing is turned into a curse for him who is promoted to become a heretic, from which curse no one is considered a stranger, who rejoices that he has invaded the ecclesiastical ministry through the desire of profit. Whence the custom of selling episcopates to the laity proceeded, I am quite astonished, when blessed Ambrose, in his pastoral discourse, crying rather than laughing, after much subjoins: the people and the uneducated, who learned such a priest for themselves. If you wish to inquire faithfully who presided over them as priests, they will soon answer and say: I was recently ordained by the archbishop, and I gave him a hundred solids, that I might have merited the episcopal favor; which if I had not given at all, I should not be a bishop to-day: wherefore it is better for me to bring in gold from the chapel, than to lose so much of the priesthood. I gave gold, and procured the episcopate; which, however, if I live, I do not doubt that I will immediately receive the solid ones. I ordain priests, consecrate deacons, and receive gold; for, nevertheless, I am confident that I will continue to make money in other respects. Behold, the gold which I gave, I received in my chapel; I therefore received the episcopate gratis. Of course, this is what I regret, because the archbishop carnally made a bishop: for because of money he specially ordained a leper: Money, he says, be with you for destruction (Acts 8:20), because you bought the gift of the Holy Spirit at a price of grace, and you carried on a miserable trade in the destruction of souls. With what mind the holy man said this, it is easy to understand from what precedes and what follows.

But those who are called Simonians joined in the cursing of their laity, as was done by the example of the priests, who joined Pilate and Herod, the leaders of their race, to the ministry of Passion Sunday. Nor is it hidden from us that for bishops of this kind, who are chosen not for the merit of life or for the teaching of wisdom, but rather for the greatest sum of money, the seed of discord and loss increases in the kingdom, according to the witness of Gregory, written in the Epistle to the kings Theodebert and Theoderic: The Simoniac heresy, which first crept up against the Church by diabolical planting, and in its very rise was smitten and condemned by the weapon of apostolic vengeance, is to be dominated in the limits of your kingdom; since in priests faith is to be chosen with life. From this, not only is a fatal wound inflicted on the soul of the organizer and the ordained, but also the guilt of your excellency's kingdom of bishops, whose intercessions should have been helped, is aggravated. And then: "Therefore, it is to be feared that there will be a greater calamity for those places where such intercessors are brought to the place of government, who will provoke God's anger in themselves more than they should have appeased the people by themselves." Nor does our care suffer this evil to be neglected, that some, drawn by the instinct of empty glory, suddenly seize the honor of the priesthood from the habit of a layman, and, as it is shameful to say, and it is heavy to keep silent, the rulers of the rulers, and those who are to be taught, the teachers, should not be ashamed to be seen, nor be afraid." Hitherto St. Gregory. And when prelates of this kind, intent on avarice, allow the churches to be utterly destroyed, and destroy by their example the manners of their subjects, whom they ought to have corrected, it remains that the defenders of the churches, and their founders, and the heirs of the founders, withdraw from their communion, that they may not be partakers of the curse. Nevertheless, if the pontifical sublimity and the royal majesty are catholic, the authority of both weighs in equal proportion, so that they may benefit the Church which Christ redeemed with his blood; for he declares his sublimity to the people spiritually by the law of the Lord, than he commends his majesty, if necessary, by the defense of arms: therefore it is necessary to be careful that they do not break away from each other, whose respective ministries agree. But their concord in various offices consults for itself as much as it feels that by consulting with one accord it is of common interest. For this reason, the names of emperors or consuls are prefixed to the pages of the ancient councils, whose favor was held by the great bishops, who always first carefully discussed the purity of the faith, whom they found worthy of the council from the order. Wherefore, most pious, according to the manner of your predecessors, give your assent to those councils by which the state is improved and increased by reconciliation; for if in any conciliatory manner the estates or possessions of another wish to ascribe to themselves the other's private affairs, and therefore, to the detriment of the brother, by collecting money through coffers and pockets, to quench the thirst of his avarice, without observing the triennial law which emanated from the constitution of the princes or the authority of the canons, you know beyond a doubt that this evil regards you, who therefore hold the summit of the kingdom, that you may execute just judgment upon all. For you, our masters, each one of his subjects cries out to God and says: God, give your judgment to the king, and your justice to the king's son: to judge your people in justice, and your poor in judgment (Ps. 71:1, 2). Although the meaning of these verses may be referred to God the Father of all and his only-begotten Son, yet there is nothing to prevent it from being understood to be prayed for an earthly king, that he may judge the people not by his own but by the judgment of God, to whom he is going to give an account even of his idle word.

Nor do I submit myself to the examination of your and other sages: those whom I suspect have felt against the canons, I accuse of having moved the hand of the bishops of the monks, I blaspheme of having taken away your benevolence from their own bishop, I accuse them of having participated in certain excommunications. But be. Whose opinion of the canons did I contradict, who could scarcely see the book opened in any council? or that there was that council, where they came reconciled and went back discordant, when there the dissidents had to be reconciled, or to be fined by the canonical division? What did the bishops commit to me singularly, that I should at least be willing to obey them in thought; especially when it happened that not an enemy, but a close friend in faith and work had endured grave dangers? Behold, I do not lie before God in Christ (Gal. 1:20), because, having heard the exclamation of those who followed, I moved beyond what can be said, remembering the former friendship and benefits of such a man, whose snow on the head shows reverence, except for the prerogatives of the primacy and the priestly insignia. By what suggestion did I deceive you, that you should take away your good-will from the best, and bestow it on the ill-deserved? Am I God who changes minds, changes kingdoms and times? I truly confess that I am ignorant of magic, and have learned nothing of the evil arts. Wherefore he who

APOLOGY TO HUGH & ROBERT, KINGS OF FRANCE

complains against me of this matter seems to accuse no one but you, who, having abandoned the path of equity, neglected to repay the turn of his benefits. Or perhaps I despise the authority of the royal majesty! No matter how much he exasperated you, exasperated you by exasperating you, offended you by exasperating you, delayed appeasing you by offending you, and for such favors he is surprised that small gifts of just compensation were expended upon him; nor does he impute to himself what he has earned, but endeavors to transfer the crime to the destruction of the innocent: for if he thought that you had done no harm while he took ours, surely he did not believe that they were the masters of our property, nor the defenders; but if he believed, he injured you with me, and did not know that he had injured himself. Why, then, does he accuse me of declamation? Why does he impute to me alone that it burdens him? Shall I be able to know how often I have sent ambassadors, how often I have asked for peace, how often I have offered myself as an executioner? God is my witness that, in keeping with the law of our monastery, I was ready to comply with all that he had regularly enjoined, and if I did anything wrong, the abundance of things remaining unshaken, the just decision of the bishops would be shot at me; because he alone, as he should have done, would never again, except by clandestine execution, make his wrath upon me. For I know how austere he was in Letaldus the monk of Miciacens, whom he treated insultingly and without any laws, forgetting priestly reverence; who, if he had read Gregory's letter to Lupus the abbot, would surely never have committed such a deed: "Since, he says, many opportunities are sought for the deception of religious persons by wicked men there, as it is said, we do not think that the priests of the aforesaid Church should in any way be deprived and deposed, unless the cause specially requires a crime; wherefore it is necessary that, if a complaint of this kind should arise against him, the bishop of the city should not alone examine the case, but employ his co-bishops to make a careful investigation, insofar as, all judging in unison, the censure of the canonical district may either strike the guilty or acquit the innocent. "Finally, what he asserts that I mixed with the excommunicated, I certainly did by his example, who received the sons of Belial in a night of robbery to kill me, after his archbishop of singular merit, Siguinus, had anathematized them; and Odo, bishop of the Carnotians, and also other men of great life and religion. This, of course, is open to all, as he is of great authority, and he asserted that no one can excommunicate him who is intent on correction and satisfaction, especially since he and the other bishops demand a sentence of damnation until their satisfaction is adequate. Moreover, who or how many should participate in the commitment of the guilty, who or how many in their acquittal, I do not remember ever having read, except in the degradation of the priest. The evangelist only says that if your brother has sinned against you, rebuke him between you and him alone: if he listens to you, you will have won your brother; if he will not hear you, tell the Church; that if he does not listen to the Church, let him be to you like a tax collector and a tax collector (Matt. 18:15, 17). Behold the rule of divine mercy, by which we are commanded to accuse others of the guilty in secret with pious correction who hear, and to rebuke others with public invective even to the ears of the Church, who do not hear. But did the public import take away the secret indulgence, or did the secret import take away the public indulgence? Does public importation require public indulgence, and secret importation requires secret indulgence? Moreover, he who offers his gift at the altar, will he not be reconciled to me there for his crime, because he has betrayed the Church? (Matt. 5:23) O times! O morals: Surely those who want to carry out their perverted desires in the fabrications of lies, themselves strive to create new laws: but the Apostle, advising us, met them: . The book of Judges shows how much to beware of anathema, where it is read: Anathema is in your midst, O Israel, you will not be able to stand before your enemies (Jos. 7:13). For that it is not to be excommunicated lightly, and that a member of Christ is to be severed from the body with great pain, is a manifest chapter in the African council: He says to anyone that he cannot be convinced by other documents. Indeed, whatever is done in the Church, unless it is supported by the authority of the Fathers, is judged to be a sham, not the truth; and we know that if pretenders and tricksters provoke the wrath of God, will a priest or a bishop be judged, who is ordained against the authority of the canons? Or will a priest or a bishop cease from his office without authentic degradation? Shall we believe an excommunicated person who is not remorseful of the crime for which he should be deprived of communion? For then the excommunication of the shepherd is just, when the canonical call has preceded the guilty, and he has refused to correct his guilt under the judgment of the Church, and in this way he separates the swollen from the healthy sheep, whom he does not know to be separated by the divine judgment; and because he had sinned against his pastor by excommunicating him, the other neither ought nor could absolve him. Moreover, whoever inflicts excommunication on my brother who sins against me, he does not forgive his sin, but I on whom he has sinned. or the kiss of peace stuck to the banishment. Moreover, when I speak familiarly to my masters and advise them of good things, I know that the hearts of many are stirred up against me, according to the saying of the Comedians: Obedience to friends, truth begets hatred. I am not much moved by their animosity, my sweet friend, Robert, whom divine piety has brought to the pinnacle of the kingdom, having been issued by the first kings, if, after God and his saints, he is specially supported by your help and with a plan, the mention of which I never fail to mention in my daily prayers, I will finally cover in chapter by chapter what are most to be corrected in your government, and yet not these in my words, but in the authentic words of the saints, so that afterwards you may move the bishops to amend these things canonically in their councils.

At first I believed it to be said of the faith, which I heard was varied by alternate choirs both in France and in the Church of England. Others say, as I think, according to Athanasius, "The Holy Spirit was not made, nor created, nor begotten of the Father and the Son, but proceeding;" but others only, "The Holy Spirit was not made, nor created, but proceeding from the Father and the Son," who while, taking away that which is, and not begotten, they believe themselves to follow the Synod of Lord Gregory, where it is thus written: "The Holy Spirit is neither begotten nor begotten, but only proceeds." About the end of the world I also heard a discourse before the people in the church of Paris as a young man, that the Antichrist would come immediately after the end of the number of a thousand years, and that not long after the universal judgment would follow. Finally, my abbot of blessed memory, Richard, with a shrewd spirit, dispelled the error which he insinuated about the end of the world, after he had received the letters from the Lotharians, to which he commanded me to answer; for the report had almost filled the whole world, that when the Sunday Annunciation took place in Parasceve it was without any scruple the end of the age. Even about the beginning of Advent, which takes place every year before the Christmas of the Lord, sometimes there was a very serious error, while others began after the 5th month. In December, before others, when it never lasts more than four weeks, there is at least one day of Advent; and since from this kind of diversity disputes tend to grow in the Church, it must be determined by a council, that all who live in it may be of one mind, which your energy will grant, who wishes to have us of one mind in his house.

LATIN TEXT

Apologeticus ad Hugonem et Rodbertum reges Francorum

Saepe contingit ut, dum nimius insurgentium calamitatum horror mentem fatigat, ipso horrore non ea quae dicere debuerat turbatus animus expediat, sed phantasmate cogitationum aliorsum raptus, quae tacenda erant dicat, ac, quod est consequens, quae dicenda taceat. Semper enim summae tranquillitatis quietem diligit, qui veritatis arcanum ratiocinando disponere gessit: quapropter ab ipsis disciplinarum rudimentis, sicut cervus desiderat ad fontes aquarum (Psal. XLI, 1), ita desideravit anima mea laboriosum spiritalis philosophiae otium quod ad multorum utilitatem verterem in honestum negotium; sed, meis peccatis praepedientibus, eo relicto, quodammodo ad saeculi sollicitudinem sum reductus, qui sub cura pastoralis regiminis quotidie sustentor aqua angustiae et pane tribulationis (III Reg. XXII, 27): corrodit me canino dente aemulorum supplantatrix calliditas, circumlatrat adversariorum frequens acerbitas, nec aliud contra me immurmurant, nisi quod monachorum senatum salvum esse volui, nostrae reipublicae augmentum quaesivi, ac cavillationi insidiantium auctoritate qua valui contradixi, nec abscondi omnino misericordiam et veritatem a consilio multo. Pro hujusmodi malis meo insidiantur sanguini, me succenturiatis insequuntur odiis: adeo ut nec regia majestas eos deterreat quin me clanculo trucident, si eis locus tempusve arrideat. Unde sedulus in orationibus meis Deum deprecor ut judicet et discernat causam meam solito, eripiatque ab homine iniquo et doloso (Psal. XLII, 1); et, si coram dominis meis episcopis, quos catholica fide orthodoxos didici, locum defendendi accipiam, credo me innoxium futurum a crimine, si jurgiorum originem examinaverint absque personarum acceptione. Quis enim suo praejudicio ad id deveniet, ut aliqua qualiscunque monasterii possessiuncula abalienari debeat? Quis rerum extortor legumque contortor funiculos ecclesiasticae haereditatis miscendo confundere praesumat, cum scriptum sit: Ne transgrediaris terminos quos posuerunt patres tui? (Prov. XXII, 22.) Ecce, secundum regulas sanctorum Patrum, judicio episcoporum subditus audientiam non diffugio, villicationis meae rationem redditurus, tantum fide accepta ut non ab insidiantibus interceptus aliquid patiar; qui paratus sum mori, si aliquando digna morte commisi. Et primum de fide mea discutiendum exopto, sine qua salvus esse non potero, ut mea examinatione alii proficiant, vel mea obtestatione se in haeresim cecidisse cognoscant, a qua conentur quantocius erui: ne in ea usque ad mortem manendo fiant stipula diaboli; nam quicunque de Deo, de religione, de communi statu sanctae Ecclesiae aliter credit quam Christus docuit, aut sub sanctis apostolis catholica Ecclesia tenuit, suisque successoribus tenendum tradidit, non catholicus vel fidelis, sed plane haereticus existit. Siquidem omnes haereses ita persecuti sunt patres nostri, ut primitus, fide exposita, explorarent in suis conciliis ne quis sentiret aliquid contrarium ipsis apostolis, qui repertus absque ulla dilatione aut ad corpus totius Ecclesiae est reductus, aut usque ad erroris abrenuntiationem perculsus anathemate, catholica privatus est communione, nec magis serpentem tangere vitaverunt orthodoxi, quam adhaerere hujusmodi lepra contaminatis. Unde in canonibus prohibemur, si nos catholicos esse scimus, ne cum eis saltem oremus: nam sub Marciano principe apud Chalcedoniam XV et eo amplius dierum actio de hac re ventilata est, residentibus episcopis ducentis, et, ut quibusdam placet, mille ducentis, quibus omnibus pius princeps ex suorum rerum copia sumptus abundanter praebuit quoad omnes haereticos a se repellerent, id est eos qui in verbo vel opere aliter quam sancti apostoli sensissent. Quo facto, in tantum puritas fidei pio placuit principi, ut eam ipse cum sua conjuge sub chirographo hoc publice profiteretur coram illo magno concilio, cujus piam religionem imitamini, domini nostri, Hugo et Rotberte, clarissimi reges, si in terra viventium Christo vultis esse haeredes et cohaeredes, et de regno vestro omnem haereticam pravitatem depellite, ut Deus vos custodiat in aeterna pace. Sciendum quippe est quod sacerdos quotidie inter missarum solemnia non pro haereticis vel schismaticis, sed pro orthodoxis tantum atque catholicae et apostolicae fidei cultoribus Deo supplicans intercedit, a qua nimirum supplicatione alienus existit qui in verbo vel opere se ab eorum unanimitate superbiendo dividit; qui vero se peccatis obnoxium vel fide dubium humiliter confitetur, portandus et corrigendus est non ut extraneus, sed ut frater, quia nec dum partem suam posuit cum hypocritis, praesertim cum et Petrus princeps Ecclesiae Deum negaverit, et Thomas in fide dubitaverit; siquidem ex utroque sexu fidelium tres ordines, ac si tres gradus, in sancta et universali Ecclesia esse novimus; quorum licet nullus sine peccato sit, tamen primus est bonus, secundus melior, tertius est optimus. Et primus quidem ordo est in utroque sexu conjugatorum; secundus continentium, vel viduarum; tertius virginum vel sanctimonialium. Virorum tantum similiter tres sunt gradus vel ordines, quorum primus est laicorum, secundus clericorum, tertius monachorum. Sed quoniam horum graduum differentias proposui, et alium alio meliorem seu sanctiorem dicere ratum duxi, qualiter singuli in suo proposito exspectant praemium aeternae retributionis, vel qualiter sanctorum

Patrum auctoritate de suo gradu in alterum promoveri possint, breviter expediendum credidi.

Et conjugii quidem ratio sola indulgentia permittitur, ne fragilitate carnis in deterius aetas proclivior delabatur. Nulli enim conjugium interdicitur, nisi ei qui ob promerenda supernae patriae gaudia sponte sua delegit jugem continentiam, quam et si minus exhibuit, devotione secretius irrita, secretiori facinus delendum est poenitentia: ita tamen ut in eo gradu permaneat, in quo malum se perpetrasse deplorat; sin vero sacerdotum Testamenti Veteris hanc sibi defendere voluerit, proprio gradu decidens, fletibus culpam diluit. Ecce ratio: si inter eos sit quibus licet, nulla poena mulctatur, sed etiam digna praemio habetur, eo quod obediendo, castitate contenta sit quam Apostolus docuit; propterea autem adjectum est si inter eos sit quibus licitum est, quia sunt in utroque sexu qui se voto obligant ut, si virgines sunt, in virginitate permaneant; et, si virgines non sunt, spreta carnis copula in caelibatu perpetualiter vivant; est etiam cognatio vel propinquitas generis, a cujus carnali commistione prohibentur omnes qui sunt sub catholica fide. Porro inter eos qui se voto obligant, vel inter eos qui nec dum transierunt septimam generis lineam, detestabile connubium ita sub poenitentiae remedio solvendum est illico, sicut illud quod poenitentia non indiget, quia ex auctoritate licet, nunquam solvendum est, nisi aut alterius conjugum morte, aut utriusque caelibatus professione.

Hinc transitur ad continentium vel viduarum excellentiorem ordinem, in quo, secundum Apostolum, si permanserint, tanto majorem aeternae remunerationis merebuntur coronam, quanto de experta carnis voluptate graviorem sustinent poenam. His quoque per discretionem secundas nuptias indulsit, dicens quod melius esset nubere quam uri (I Cor. VII, 9). De tertiis vero vel quartis nec non et pluribus nuptiis, non me legisse memini utrum a catholicis debeant celebrari; sed hoc absque ullo scrupulo occurrit: quod si hoc facinus grave est in feminis, multo gravius est si contingat in viris.

Virginum quanta sit gloria, nullus ignorat. Quis scit hoc appetere hominem ex gratiae praerogativa, quod habet angelus ex natura? quae virtus virginitatis cum in humilitate solidatur, singularis meriti recompensatione donabitur, quia Deus repromittit virginibus quod sequantur Agnum quocunque ierit (Apoc. XIV, 4); hac virtute sanctimonialium decoratur venerabile collegium, hanc se gaudent multi per omnes viriles ordines promeruisse in gremio suae matris Ecclesiae.

Sed his posthabitis, primo de virorum ordine, id est de laicis, dicendum est, quod alii sunt agricolae, alii agonistae: et agricolae quidem insudant agriculturae et diversis artibus in opere rustico, unde sustentatur totius Ecclesiae multitudo; agonistae vero, contenti stipendiis militiae, non se collidunt in utero matris suae, verum omni sagacite expugnant adversarios sanctae Dei Ecclesiae.

Sequitur clericorum ordo, qui in tribus gradibus specialiter distinguitur, hoc est, diaconorum, presbyterorum et episcoporum: nam omnes qui sunt inferioris gradus per abusionem clerici vocantur, dum eis sicut et laicis ex indulgentia permittitur sociari conjugibus. Constat sane ab apostolis et eorum successoribus esse prohibitum clericos, id est diaconos, presbyteros et episcopos esse uxorios. Κλῆρος etenim Graece, Latine dicitur sors, unde clerici ad sacrificandum vel ad ministrandum in sortem Dei adsciti studeant non carnaliter sed spiritualiter filios gignere, ut semper sint memores sortis sanctorum in lumine; nam ipsi quotidiana sollicitudine omnium Ecclesiarum suscepta (II Cor. II, 28) in activa vita laborant cum Martha quae turbatur erga plurima (Luc. X, 41). Porro illud unum quod est necessarium in contemplativa vita adepti monachi, cum Maria tanto magis delectantur pedes Jesu lacrymis rigare et capillis tergere (Luc. VII, 38), quanto remotiores sunt ab omnium negotiorum saeculi inquietudine: siquidem clericorum ordo inter laicos et monachos medius, quantum est superior inferiore, tantum inferior superiore, quandoquidem quo discrepat ab utroque ordinum jungitur ad alterutrum. Illi namque sunt conjugibus colligati, rei familiaris curae dediti, saeculi actibus occupati: isti a saeculi actibus alieni, propriae voluntati abrenuntiando, Patris spiritualis imperiis obsequendo, qui et eleemosyna bonorum virorum et labore manuum suarum vivunt, et possunt dicere cum Petro: Ecce nos reliquimus omnia, et secuti sumus te (Matth. XIX, 27). Denique clericorum vita irreprehensibilis speculum est totius Ecclesiae, sicut monachorum habitus et professio firma exemplum est totius summae poenitentiae; et quamvis clerici reprehensione digni, ne tractent sancta profani, degradentur certis ex causis, monachi tamen nisi causa superbiae nunquam privantur ex toto fratrum suorum communione, cum et criminosos laicos vel clericos suscipiant, et se in crimine deprehensos regulari disciplina corripiant. Denique ex monachis presbyter ordinatus, vel ex clerico monachus factus sciat se non clericorum more ecclesiasticis officiis deservire, sed Gregoriani privilegii institutione missas celebret in congregatione. Verum quia de singulis ordinibus quae videbantur dicta sunt, qualiter alterius in alterum promotio fiat tacendum non est. Promoventur namque ex laicis vel clericis ad monachatum, promoventur ex laicis vel monachis ad clericatum, quod quando vel quomodo fieri debeat sanctorum Patrum auctoritas liquido manifestat, quam qui secuti non sunt extra Ecclesiam catholicam a fide aberraverunt. Quamobrem in canone, dum orant pro orthodoxis atque catholicae et apostolicae fidei cultoribus, cavendum illis summopere est, quod papa Gregorius in suo synodo refert: Una est, inquiens, fides, unum baptisma, una Ecclesia catholica, in qua sola possint relaxari peccata. Si enim extra eam remissio peccatorum non est, haereticus vel schismaticus ut quid jejunat? ut quid decimas dat? ut quid Deum supplex adorat? Nam sicut fuit multitudinis credentium unum cor et anima una (Act. IV, 32), ita, per totum orbem terrarum, eorum omnium qui, secundum doctrinam apostolorum, unum in Deo sapiant, una est Ecclesia, quae de Graeco in Latinum convocatio interpretatur, quia ad unam fidem et ad unum baptisma omnes vocamur. Quapropter unaquaeque domus ubi erecto altari populus ad Deum supplicandum convenit, dum habeat nomen ecclesiae, veneratione et summo honore digna est in omni gente, quoniam in ea renascimur ex aqua et Spiritu sancto (Joan. III, 5), in ea divina celebrantur mysteria, in ea fit confessio et remissio peccatorum. Caveat igitur quicunque vult salvus esse eam alicujus, nisi solius Dei, possessionem credere; unde Petro apostolorum principi dicitur: Tu es Petrus, et super hanc petram aedificabo Ecclesiam meam (Matth. XVI, 18). Meam inquit, non tuam; et Christus alibi: Domus mea, domus orationis vocabitur (Matth. XXI, 13). Psalmista quoque: Domum tuam, Domine, decet sanctitudo (Psal. XCII, 5). Si ergo Ecclesia non est Petri, cujus erit? aut successores Petri audebunt potestatem sibi vindicare, quam non habuit Petrus princeps Ecclesiae? Certe, charissimi principes, nec catholice vivimus, nec catholice loquimur, quando ego illam ecclesiam dico esse meam, ille alteram dicit esse suam, ac veluti quaedam jumenta comparati jumentis insipientibus utrasque aliquando venales proponimus, propositasque ab aliis emere non formidamus.

APOLOGY TO HUGH & ROBERT, KINGS OF FRANCE

Est etiam alius error gravissimus, quo fertur altare esse episcopi, et ecclesia alterius cujuslibet domini, cum ex domo consecrata et altari unum quiddam fiat quod dicitur ecclesia, sicut unus homo constat ex corpore et anima. Videte, aequissimi principes, quo nos ducit cupiditas, dum refrigescit charitas (Matth. XXIV, 12); ex donis omnipotentis Dei, quae gratis accipiuntur, mercatores efficimur, et vendere conamur quod profecto non possidemus. Nihil enim pene ad Ecclesiam, quae est solius Dei, pertinere videtur quod ad pretium non largiatur, scilicet episcopatus, presbyteratus, diaconatus, et reliqui minores gradus, archidiaconatus quoque, decania, praepositura, thesauri custodia, baptisterium, sepultura, et si qua sunt similia. Et hujusmodi negotiatores subdola responsione solent astruere non se emere benedictionem qua percipitur gratia Spiritus sancti, sed res Ecclesiarum, vel possessiones episcopi, cum certum sit quod in catholica Ecclesia alterum altero carere non possit. An aliquis usus est igne sine ea, qua nutritur, fomenti materia? aut ignem aliquando tenuit, et calore caruit? Quis mel sine dulcedine? quis absinthium sine amaritudine deprehendit? Attamen eamdem aquam diverso tenore dulcem et amaram est inveniri possibile; quod, quia ex contingenti fit, aliquando nostram opinionem fallit, ut, quae creditur dulcis, amara existat. Sic quoque talis negotiatio bona aestimatur, cum pro certo mala sit, quia turpis lucri gratia contingit: de qua re adeo consuetudo inolevit, ut hoc jam credatur sine peccato fieri. Verum Spiritus sanctus per os beati papae Gregorii dicit: Quia benedictio illi in maledictionem vertitur qui ad hoc ut fiat haereticus promovetur, a qua maledictione nullus extraneus habetur, qui lucri cupiditate se ministerium ecclesiasticum invasisse laetatur (L. VII, Epist. 3). Unde vero processerit usus ut laici vendant episcopatus, satis demiror, cum beatus Ambrosius in sermone pastorali, flendo, potius quam ridendo, post multa subjungat: « Videas, inquiens, in Ecclesia passim quos non merita, sed pecuniae, ad episcopatus ordinem provexerunt: nugacem populum et indoctum, qui talem sibi adsciverunt sacerdotem. Quos si percontari fideliter velis quis eos praefecerit sacerdotes, respondebunt mox, et dicent: Ab archiepiscopo sum nuper ordinatus, centumque ei solidos dedi, ut episcopalem gratiam consequi meruissem; quos si minime dedissem, hodie episcopus non essem: unde melius mihi est aurum de sacello invehere, quam tantum sacerdotium perdere. Aurum dedi, et episcopatum comparavi; quos tamen solidos, si vivo, recepturum me illico non diffido. Ordino presbyteros, consecro diaconos, et accipio aurum; nam et de aliis ordinibus nihilominus pecuniae quaestum profligare confido. Ecce et aurum, quod dedi, in meo sacello recepi; episcopatum igitur gratis accepi. Nempe hoc est quod doleo, quia archiepiscopus carnaliter episcopum fecit: nam propter pecunias specialiter leprosum ordinavit: Pecunia, inquit, tecum sit in perditionem (Act. VIII, 20), quia donum sancti Spiritus gratiae pretio comparasti, et commercium miserabile in animarum exitium peregisti (Lib. De dignitate sacerdotali, cap. 5). » Haec sanctus vir quo animo dixerit, ex praecedentibus et consequentibus facile datur intelligi.

Quod vero illi qui dicuntur Simoniaci laicos suae immiscuerunt maledictioni, exemplo factum est sacerdotum, qui ad ministerium Dominicae passionis adjunxerunt sibi Pilatum et Herodem principes suae gentis. Nec illud nos latet quod pro hujuscemodi episcopis, qui non pro vitae merito vel sapientiae doctrina, sed magis eliguntur pro pecuniarum summa maxima, discordiarum semen et detrimentum regno accrescat, teste Gregorio, in Epistola ad Theodebertum et Theodericum reges scripta: « Fertur, inquit, Simoniacam haeresim, quae prima contra Ecclesiam diabolica plantatione subrepsit, et in ipso ortu suo telo apostolicae ultionis percussa atque damnata est, in regni vestri finibus dominari; cum in sacerdotibus fides sit eligenda cum vita. » Et post pauca: « Hinc non solum in ordinatoris et ordinati animam lethale vulnus infigitur, verum etiam excellentiae vestrae regnum episcoporum culpa, quorum intercessionibus juvari debuerat, praegravatur. » Ac deinde: « Major ergo metuenda est locis illis fore calamitas, ubi tales intercessores ad locum regiminis adducuntur, qui Dei in se magis iracundiam provocent, quam per semetipsos populis placare debuerant. Nec hoc quoque malum sollicitudo nostra patitur negligenter omittere, quod quidam, instinctu gloriae inanis illecti ex laico repente habitu sacerdotii honorem arripiunt, et, quod dicere pudet et grave tacere est, regendi rectores, et qui docendi sunt doctores, nec erubescant videri, nec metuant (l. IX, Epist. 110). » Huc usque S. Gregorius. Cumque hujusmodi praelati avaritiae intenti ecclesias funditus dirui sinant, mores subjectorum suo exemplo perdant, quos corrigere debuerant, restat ut defensores ecclesiarum ac fundatores earum haeredesque fundatorum se subtrahant eorum communioni, ne participes sint maledictionis. Verumtamen si catholica sit pontificialis sublimitas et regalis majestas, aequa lance pensat utriusque auctoritas, ut prosint Ecclesiae quam Christus redemit suo sanguine; nam illius sublimitas lege Domini spiritaliter populis pronuntiat, quam istius majestas, si necesse sit, armorum defensione commendat: quapropter cavendum est ne ab invicem resiliant, quorum adinvicem ministeria concordant. Sed concordia eorum in diversis officiis tanto sibi consulit, quanto unanimiter consulendo de communi utilitate sentit. Ob hoc antiquorum conciliorum paginis praefiguntur nomina imperatorum vel consulum quorum favore magnorum habita sunt consulta episcoporum, qui semper prius diligenter discusserunt de fidei puritate, quos concilio dignos reperirent ex ordine. Quamobrem, piissimi, more praedecessorum vestrorum regum illis assensum praebete conciliis quibus per reconciliationem res publica melioratur et crescit; quia, si quocunque conciliabulo alterius praedia vel possessiunculas alter privatis negotiis velit sibi adscribere, ac ideo, fratris damno, pecuniam per arcas et loculos aggregando, sitim suae avaritiae exstinguere, non observata tricennali lege quae emanavit ex constitutione principum seu auctoritate canonum, sciatis procul dubio quod ad vos hoc malum respicit, qui idcirco regni apicem tenetis, ut justum judicium omnibus faciatis. Pro vobis nimirum dominis nostris unusquisque subjectorum ad Deum clamat et dicit: Deus, judicium tuum regi da, et justitiam tuam filio regis: judicare populum tuum in justitia, et pauperes tuos in judicio (Psal. LXXI, 1, 2). Quorum versuum sensus quamvis referri possit ad Deum Patrem omnium Filiumque ejus unigenitum, tamen nihil obest intelligi de terreno rege precari, ut judicet populum non suo sed Dei judicio, cui rationem redditurus est etiam de otioso verbo.

Nec me vestro aliorumque sapientium examini subduco: qui contra canones sensisse suspicor, in episcopos monachorum manum movisse accusor, vestram benevolentiam proprio episcopo abstulisse blasphemor, quibusdam excommunicatis participasse criminor. Sed esto. Cui sententiae canonum contradixi, qui nullo concilio vix apertum librum videre potui? aut quod concilium illud fuit, ubi conciliati venerunt et disconciliati recesserunt, cum ibi discordes reconciliari debuerint, aut canonica districtione mulctari? quid in me singulariter commiserunt episcopi, ut eis saltem cogitatione obesse voluerim; praesertim cum non inimicum, sed fide et opere amicissimum graviora pericula pertulisse contigerit? Ecce coram Deo in Christo non mentior (Gal. I, 20), quia, audita insequentium conclamatione, ultra quam dici possit indolui, recordatus pristinae amicitiae et beneficiorum tanti viri, cujus nix capitis reverendum ostendit, excepta primatis praerogativa et sacerdotali infula. Qua suggestione vos decepi, ut vestram benevolentiam optimis auferretis, male meritis conferretis? Num ego Deus sum qui mutat mentes, mutat regna et tempora? Vere fateor me magicam ignorare, nec aliquid malarum artium didicisse. Unde ille qui de hac re contra me queritur, neminem praeter vos incusare videtur, qui, relicto tramite aequitatis, beneficiorum ejus vicissitudinem rependere neglexistis. Aut fortasse regiae majestatis auctoritatem contemno! Quantulumcunque vos exacerbavit, exacerbando irritavit, irritando offendit, offendendo placare distulit, et pro talibus beneficiis miratur sibi impendi munuscula justae recompensationis; nec sibi imputat quod promeruit, sed crimen transferre nititur in perniciem insontis: si enim nihil vos nocuisse putavit, dum nostra tulit, profecto nec dominos nostrarum rerum esse, nec defensores credidit; si autem credidit, vos mecum laesit, nec se laesisse ignoravit. Cur igitur me declamatorie accusat? cur mihi soli imputat quod illum gravat? An scire potero, quoties legatos misi, quoties de pace rogavi, quoties me supplicem obtuli? Testis mihi est Deus quod, salvo jure nostri monasterii, ad omnia quae regulariter injunxisset obtemperare paratus fui, et, si aliquid mali commerui, manente rerum copia inconcussa, episcoporum justa jaculetur in me sententia; quia ipse solus, ut debuerat, nunquam justo amplius, nisi clandestina exsecutione, in me desaeviet. Novi enim quam austerus in Letaldo Miciacensi monacho fuerit, quem oblitus reverentiae sacerdotalis injuriose et sine ullis legibus tractavit; qui si epistolam Gregorii ad Lupum abbatem legisset, profecto nunquam tantum facinus perpetrasset: « Quoniam multae, inquit, occasiones in deceptatione religiosarum personarum a pravis illic, ut dicitur, hominibus exquiruntur, presbyterum praedictae Ecclesiae nullomodo privandum deponendumque censemus, nisi causa specialiter criminis exigente; unde necesse est ut, si qua contra eum hujusmodi querela surrexerit, non solus episcopus civitatis causam examinet, sed adhibitis sibi coepiscopis suis subtili investigatione perquirat, quatenus, cunctis concorditer judicantibus, canonicae districtionis censura aut reum ferire aut innocentem possit absolvere. » Denique quod excommunicatis me miscuisse asserit, ejus exemplo utique feci, qui filios Belial nocturno latrocinio in meam necem grassantes recepit, postquam eos anathematizaverat suus archiepiscopus singularis meriti Siguinus; et Odo Carnotensium episcopus, nec non et alii magnae vitae et religiosi viri. Hoc sane palam omnibus, sicut magnae auctoritatis est, asseruit quod nemo possit eum excommunicare, qui emendationi et satisfactioni intendit, praesertim cum usque ad satisfactionem congruam suam ipse et alii episcopi praetendant maledictionis sententiam. Porro qui vel quot interesse debeant reorum obligationi, qui vel quot eorum absolutioni, nusquam me legisse memini, nisi in degradatione sacerdotis. Tantum evangelicus sermo prodit quod si peccaverit in te frater tuus, corripe eum inter te et ipsum solum: si te audierit, lucratus eris fratrem tuum; si te non audierit, dic Ecclesiae; quod si Ecclesiam non audierit, sit tibi sicut ethnicus et publicanus (Matth. XVIII, 15, 17). Ecce divinae miserationis regula, qua jubemur reorum alios audientes pia correctione secretius arguere, alios non audientes publica invectione objurgare usque ad aures Ecclesiae. Sed nunquid publica invectio secretam indulgentiam sustulit, aut secreta invectio publicam indulgentiam ademit? An publica invectio publicam indulgentiam, et secreta invectio secretam indulgentiam requirit? Porro qui offert munus suum ad altare, non ibi reconciliabitur mihi pro scelere, quia proditus est Ecclesiae? (Matth. V, 23.) O tempora! o mores: Certe qui volunt exsequi in fabrateria mendacii cupiditates suas pravas, ipsi nituntur condere leges novas: sed Apostolus nobis consulens eis occurrit: Si quis vobis, inquiens, aliud annuntiaverit praeter id quod accepistis, anathema sit (Gal., I, 9). Quod anathema quantum cavendum sit, liber Judicum ostendit, ubi legitur: Anathema in medio tui est, Israel, non poteris stare coram inimicis tuis (Josue VII, 13). Nam quod leviter excommunicandum non sit, et quod membrum Christi a corpore cum gravi dolore resecandum sit, manifestum in concilio Africano caput est: « Quandiu, inquit, excommunicato non communicaverit suus episcopus, eidem episcopo ab aliis non communicetur episcopis, ut magis caveat episcopus ne dicat in quemquam quod aliis documentis convincere non potest. » Siquidem quidquid in Ecclesia fit, nisi auctoritate Patrum fulciatur, simulatio, non veritas judicatur; et scimus si qua simulatores et callidi provocant iram Dei, an presbyter vel episcopus habebitur, qui contra auctoritatem canonum ordinatur? Aut sine authentica degradatione presbyter vel episcopus cessabit ab officii sui munere? Nunquid credemus excommunicatum quem non remordet conscientia criminis pro quo debeat communione privari? Tunc enim justa est excommunicatio pastoris, quando canonica vocatio in reum praecessit, et ille reatum suum sub judicio Ecclesiae corrigere noluit, eoque modo elatione tumidum a sanis ovibus segregat, quem divino judicio segregandum non ignorat; et quia in suum pastorem excommunicatus peccaverat, eum alter absolvere nec debuit nec potuit. Porro quicunque fratri meo in me peccanti excommunicationem intorserit, non ille ei peccatum dimittit, sed ego in quem peccavit, a quo excommunicationis malo regnum vestrum purgate, serenissimi principes, quia vix est in eo aliquis hominum qui saltem idcirco excommunicatus non sit, quoniam in convivio vel pacis osculo excommunicato adhaesit. Praeterea dominos meos cum familiariter alloquens bona suadeo, multorum animos, scio, contra me concito, juxta illud Comici: Obsequium amicos, veritas odium parit. (TERENTIUS in

Andria, Act. I, scen. v. 1.) De quorum animositate non multum moveor, dulce decus meum, Rodberte, quem atavis regibus editum divina pietas perduxit ad regni fastigium, si post Deum et sanctos ejus vestro specialiter sustenter auxilio et consilio, cujus mentionem in quotidianis orationibus meis nunquam praetereo, tandem capitulatim subtexam huic indiculo quae maxime sunt corrigenda in vestro imperio, nec tamen haec verbis meis, sed authenticis sanctorum dictis, ut postmodum episcopos moveatis haec canonice emendare in suis conciliis.

Primitus de fide dicendum credidi, quam alternantibus choris et in Francia et apud Anglorum Ecclesiam variari audivi. Alii dicunt, ut arbitror, secundum Athanasium, « Spiritus sanctus a Patre et Filio non factus, nec creatus, nec genitus, sed procedens: » alii vero tantum, « Spiritus sanctus a Patre et Filio non factus nec creatus, sed procedens, » qui dum, id quod est, nec genitus subtrahunt, synodicam domni Gregorii se sequi credunt, ubi ita est scriptum: « Spiritus sanctus nec genitus est, nec ingenitus, sed tantum procedens. » De fine quoque mundi coram populo sermonem in Ecclesia Parisiorum adolescentulus audivi, quod statim finito mille annorum numero Antichristus adveniret, et non longo post tempore universale judicium succederet: cui praedicationi ex Evangeliis ac Apocalypsi et libro Danielis, qua potui virtute, restiti. Denique et errorem qui de fine mundi inolevit abbas meus beatae memoriae Richardus sagaci animo propulit, postquam litteras a Lothariensibus accepit, quibus me respondere jussit; nam fama pene totum mundum impleverat, quod, quando Annuntiatio Dominica in Parasceve contigisset absque ullo scrupulo finis saeculi esset. De initio etiam Adventus qui ante Nativitatem Domini per singulos annos agitur, aliquando error gravissimus exstitit, aliis inchoantibus post V Kalend. Decembris, aliis ante, cum nunquam plus quatuor hebdomadas, saltem unam diem Adventus habeat; cumque de hujusmodi diversitate soleant contentiones in Ecclesia crescere, concilio determinandum est, ut omnes qui in ea vivimus unum sapiamus, quod vestra industria concedat, qui nos unanimes vult habere in domo sua.

The Scriptorium Project is the work of a small group of lay people of various apostolic churches who are interested in the preservation, transmission, and translation of the works of the early and medieval church. Our efforts are to make the works of the church fathers accessible to anyone who might have an interest in Christian antiquities and the theological, philosophical, and moral writings that have become the bedrock of Western Civilization.

To-date, our releases have pulled from the Greek, Syriac, Georgian, Latin, Celtic, Ethiopian, and Coptic traditions of Christianity, and have been pulled from sundry local traditions and languages.

Other Selections from the Early Frankish Church Series:

Apology to Hugh & Robert, Kings of France by St. Abbo of Fleury (Nov. 2006)
Frankish & Visigothic Councils: 549-615 AD (June 2007)
Letter to Brunhilda of Austrasia by St. Germain of Paris (Sept. 2010)
The Spiritual Combat by St. Bernard of Clairvaux (Dec. 2010)
In Praise of the New Chivalry by St. Bernard of Clairvaux (Jan. 2011)
Testament by St. Burgundofara the Abbess (Jan. 2016)
Laws of the Monastery and the Church by Theuderic III, King of Franks (Feb. 2016)
The Life of King Sigebert II by Sigebert of Gembloux (Mar. 2016)
Two Letters from a Gallic Patrician by Dynamius the Patrician (July 2016)
Life of St. Germain by St. Venantius Fortunatus (Aug. 2016)
Three Letters from the Companion of the Bulgars by St. Rupert of Juvavum (Aug. 2017)
An Account of the Gallican Liturgy by St. Germain of Paris (June 2018)
Preludes by Photius of Paris (Nov. 2018)
The Privileges of Rome by Louis I the Pious, Frankish Emperor (Apr. 2019)
Edicts of the Synod of Paris by Chlothar II, King of Franks (Aug. 2019)
Laws of the Church (Ecclesiasticae Praeceptiones) by Chlothar III, King of Franks (Apr. 2020)
Laws of the Church (Ecclesiasticae Praeceptiones) by St. Dagobert II, King of Franks (Sept. 2020)
Letters of Paulinus by St. Paulinus of Aquileia (Aug. 2021)
The Italian Diplomas by Charlemagne, Holy Roman Emperor (Apr. 2023)

www.ingramcontent.com/pod-product-compliance
Lightning Source LLC
LaVergne TN
LVHW051923060526
838201LV00060B/4150